There's a Girl in My Hammerlock

adapted from the novel
by Jerry Spinelli

SCHOLASTIC INC.
New York Toronto London Auckland Sydney
Mexico City New Delhi Hong Kong

Cover illustration and interior illustrations by Don Stewart

"There's a Girl in My Hammerlock" adapted from THERE'S A GIRL IN MY HAMMERLOCK by Jerry Spinelli. Copyright © 1991 by Jerry Spinelli. Play adaptation originally published in *Scholastic Scope* magazine, October 15, 1993. Play adaptation copyright © 1993 by Scholastic Inc. Reprinted by permission of Simon & Schuster Books for Young Readers, an imprint of Simon & Schuster Children's Publishing Division.

"Wheel Trouble" by Patrick Daley and Chuck Ranberg from *Scholastic Action* magazine, January 15, 1993. Copyright © 1993 by Scholastic Inc. All rights reserved.

Compilation copyright © 2001 by Scholastic Inc.
Illustrations copyright © 2001 by Scholastic Inc.
All rights reserved. Published by Scholastic Inc.
Printed in the U.S.A.

ISBN 0-439-31286-8

4   5   6   7   8   9   10   23   10 09 08

Characters

Narrator, Maisie recalling the events

Maisie, 13, an athlete

Miss Strickland, cheerleading coach

John, Maisie's older brother

Mrs. Potter, Maisie's mom

Eric Delong, a wrestler

Liz Lampley, a cheerleader

Mr. Cappelli, a wrestling coach

Mr. Potter, Maisie's dad

Principal, of Maisie's school

Holly, Maisie's friend

George Bamberger, a wrestler

Kruko, star wrestler

Tina McIntyre, a basketball player

P.K., Maisie's little sister

Coach, of another team

Scene 1

Narrator: It was the end of the first week of school. Miss Strickland was finally posting the list of girls who'd made cheerleader. I'd been the best in try-outs. But when I ran to look at the bulletin board, my name wasn't on the list.

Maisie *(to herself)*: I can't believe it!

Narrator: Then, I spotted Miss Strickland leaving school and ran after her.

Maisie *(upset)*: Miss Strickland! My name's not on the list! There must have been a mistake!

Miss Strickland: There was no mistake, Maisie. Forty-six girls tried out, and we had spots for only five.

Maisie *(suspicious)*: Who voted against me?

Narrator: I knew that cheerleaders already on the squad voted for new members.

Miss Strickland: Maisie, you know I can't answer that.

Narrator: She got in her car and drove off.

Maisie *(shouting at the car):* It was Liz Lampley, wasn't it? I know it was her!

Why did Maisie expect to make the cheerleading squad?

Scene 2

Narrator: At dinner that night, I was still angry.

Maisie: Why didn't I make it? I was the best!

John: That's easy—you're ugly.

Narrator: Later I sat in my room with Mom.

Maisie *(upset):* My brother's right. I'm ugly.

Mrs. Potter: Where have I been? I didn't even know I had an ugly child!

Maisie: Maybe it's because I don't wear make-up. I'm not the Lizard Lampley type.

Mrs. Potter: Why don't you just go out for hockey again? You enjoyed it last year.

Maisie: I did like it, but it's time to move on. Every great woman was a cheerleader once.

Mrs. Potter: I wasn't.

Maisie: You don't count. Mom, you have to help me. You can teach me to use makeup. Then I'll go see Miss Strickland. She'll say, "Whoa! I think we can find space for another cheerleader!"

Mrs. Potter: I wouldn't want you to lower yourself like that.

Maisie: Then I'm doomed. Maisie Potter: Cut from cheerleading. Cut from life.

Mrs. Potter *(gently):*   Maisie, there's something you aren't telling me, isn't there?

Maisie: Huh? Uh, no.

Narrator: But there was something else. His name was Eric Delong.

How would you describe Maisie?

Scene 3

Narrator: Eric had changed my life the summer before. One day at the swimming pool, he accidentally bumped into me underwater. He came up, dripping wet, and spoke the words I'll never forget.

Eric: Oh, sorry.

Narrator: I was taken completely by surprise. I'd never felt like this before. I was amazed. I was in love.

Maisie *(awestruck):* Oh, that's OK.

Narrator: Then he swam away. Eric was a year ahead of me in school and a big athlete. I didn't even tell my friend Holly I was in love. Then, the second day of school, I saw Eric at the water fountain.

Maisie: Hi, Eric!

Eric: Hi.

Narrator: A moment later, he was gone. But then Lizard Lampley oozed by, smiling her rattlesnake smile.

Liz: I didn't know you liked him too.

Maisie *(playing dumb):* Like? Who?

Liz: Eric. Who else? Remember? Three seconds ago? The water fountain?

Maisie: I'm not allowed to say hello?

Liz: Not that way.

Narrator: Then she slithered away. When she got to the door, she turned to me.

Liz: Are you going out for hockey again, Maisie?

Maisie: What's it to you?

Liz: I was just thinking. It's too bad we don't cheer for hockey like we do for football. I'll be cheering right behind Eric all season. They made him quarterback, you know—because he makes such good passes.

Narrator: That was when I decided to try out for cheerleader.

How do you think Liz feels about Eric?

Scene 4

Narrator: In the end, I never was a cheerleader. I did play field hockey, and I had a great season. But a few days after it ended, I ran into Eric and Liz.

Liz: Going out for basketball, Maisie?

Maisie: Maybe.

Liz: Eric's going out for wrestling. I love those sexy wrestling suits.

Narrator: I told myself I didn't care about Eric anymore. And if I did care, there was nothing I could do about it. But the next day after school, I found myself in room 116. I kept asking myself, "Why am I here?" Other kids stared at me. Then the coach came in.

Cappelli: Gentlemen, welcome to wrestling.

Narrator: After dinner that night, my brother came storming into my room.

John: Kruko just called me. I know what you did. You're not funny.

Narrator: Kruko was our star wrestler,

Maisie: Who says I was trying to be funny?

John *(angry):* Get yourself over to girls' basketball, where you belong.

Narrator: But I didn't. The next day, I went to the wrestling room again. It was almost like being in a trance. This time the coach handed me a note.

Cappelli: Potter, give this note to your parents. I'd like to meet with the three of you.

Narrator: We met that night. The principal was there, too.

Principal: You played girls' basketball last year, didn't you, Maisie?

Maisie: Yeah. But I wanted to try something new this year. So I went out for wrestling.

Mr. Potter *(to the principal):* Is she allowed?

Principal: The law says that since there's no girls' wrestling team, she may try out for the boys' team. The real question is—do you say she's allowed?

Mrs. Potter *(to Maisie):* Do you really want to wrestle?

Maisie: I do.

Mr. Potter *(sighing):* She's allowed.

Cappelli: I've never had a girl try out before. And I don't want one now. But I won't try to stop her. Some coaches would make her so miserable, she'd quit.

Mr. Potter: But you wouldn't do that, would you, Mr. Cappelli?

Cappelli: No, I wouldn't. But I have the toughest workouts around.

Mrs. Potter: Maisie wouldn't have it any other way.

Principal: Maisie's problems don't end in the gym. Other students can be harsh.

Mrs. Potter: OK. Let's get this settled. Maisie, do you realize the situations you could get into? On the mat? Wrestling with boys?

Maisie: Yeah.

Mrs. Potter: And the kinds of things they might say? Or other people might think?

Maisie: Yes.

Mrs. Potter: Do you care?

Maisie: No.

Mrs. Potter *(to the coach):* Maisie doesn't quit. Nobody is as strong in the heart as this little girl right here.

What do you think people will say about Maisie if she joins the boys' wrestling team?

Scene 5

Narrator: I was back at practice the next day. I was in the 105-pound class. When we did sit-ups, I kept up fine. After that, Mr. Cappelli showed us how to do the referee's position. I practiced with George Bamberger, another 105-pounder. When he wrapped his arm around my waist, I started giggling.

Cappelli: Potter! What's so funny?

Maisie: Um. It . . . uh . . . tickled?

Cappelli: Potter, stand up. Give me five laps around the school. And if you want to run on home, nobody's going to stop you!

Narrator: When I got back to the gym, Mr. Cappelli looked surprised to see me. He made me do lots more sit-ups and push-ups. Later,

in the locker room I stood on the scale. I was down to 103. The next morning, I was so sore and tired that my mother had to drag me out of bed. When I got to school, things got even worse. Holly nabbed me.

Holly *(hurt):* You went out for wrestling? Are you crazy? Why didn't you tell me? I'm supposed to be your best friend! And I have to hear about this from 50 other people! I feel like such a jerk!

Maisie *(sarcastic):* I'm sorry. From now on, every time I do something, I'll get your permission. Then you won't feel like a jerk.

Holly *(angry):* Don't you care what other people think?

Maisie: No. Why do you? Huh?

Holly *(yelling):* I don't! But I learned your dirty little secret.

Maisie: Want to tell me about it? I didn't know I had one.

Holly: Eric Delong! Your good buddy Liz Lampley told me. Are you that desperate? Chasing him onto the wrestling team?

Narrator: I had nothing to say. So I just stomped off.

Do you think Maisie should have told Holly? Why or why not?

Scene 6

Narrator: At practice that day, Mr. Cappelli told us to work on the referee's position. So I paired up with Bamberger again. We wound up joking around. The coach didn't like it.

Cappelli: Bamberger and Potter! Five laps, 20 push-ups, and into my office!

Narrator: We did as he said. Then we went in to see the coach.

Cappelli *(to Bamberger):* Get out of here.

Narrator: George left.

Cappelli: What game are you playing? It's clear to me that you're a fake, a troublemaker. You don't want to wrestle. You want attention: The girl who wrestles boys.

Maisie: But...

Cappelli: Listen. Your days are numbered. Law or no law, I pick my team. Go home to your family and friends. On Monday, be at girls' basketball. Not here.

Narrator: I went home. Holly was supposed to sleep over that night, but she didn't show up. Later, Dad got a call from the father of another wrestler. He said he'd pull his kid off the team if I didn't quit.

Maisie *(depressed):* It's OK. I'm quitting anyway.

Narrator: I thought that if I quit, maybe things would go back to normal. Maybe I could get my best friend back.

Mrs. Potter: Honey, it's your decision.

Narrator: On Monday, I went to school planning to quit. Then I saw Bamberger moping by the bulletin boards.

Maisie: Hey, George. You're going to be late for practice.

George: I'm not going. I'm quitting.

Maisie: Is it because he yelled at you? *(pause)* It's not because of me, is it?

George *(beginning to smile):* Nah. You're not a problem.

Narrator: I don't know what came over me. I guess I just wanted to encourage him.

Maisie: You are not quitting, George. I won't let you.

George: It's not up to you. It's up to me.

Maisie: You're not quitting because I'm not quitting. I was. But now I'm not. I just found one person who says I'm not a problem. And I'm going to keep him. Come on. We're going to practice.

George: No. I don't want to.

Maisie: George, we need each other. We can't quit wrestling just like that. What's next? School? Life?

Narrator: Neither of us quit. And at the end of the week, the coach announced final cuts. I made the team! After I saw the list, I ran up to Mr. Cappelli.

Maisie: I really made the team? It's not a mistake?

Cappelli: I'll tell you a secret. You made the team when you came in after I told you to forget it.

Narrator: I couldn't wait to tell my family. Mom gave me a kiss. Dad shook my hand. My brother was a jerk. My little sister was proud. That was Friday. On Saturday, I went to the gym to shoot baskets. Eric and Liz were there. So was Holly, who hadn't spoken to me since our fight. I got into a game of H-O-R-S-E with Eric and won. When I got home, Holly called me.

Holly: You're so stupid. You don't know anything about guys. You don't go beating them in sports if you want them to like you. Besides, Eric loves Liz.

Narrator: I could tell that someone else was on the other extension with Holly. I suspected it was Lizard.

Maisie: Hey, Lizard. Is that you?

Narrator: The phone went click. Twice. I had definitely lost my best friend.

How do you think Maisie feels about Holly and Liz becoming friends?

Scene 7

Narrator: Once Mr. Cappelli had picked the team, we really started learning to wrestle. I hardly ever lost. I figured I had a knack for it. George didn't want to wrestle me, though. I guessed he was mad that Mr. Cappelli picked me to be varsity and him to be backup. But I was still miserable.

Mrs. Potter: What's the matter, honey? Is it Holly? I haven't seen her around lately.

Maisie: She dumped me.

Narrator: I wound up telling Mom everything—even about Eric Delong.

Mrs. Potter: Is he why you went out for wrestling?

Maisie: That's what everyone at school thinks, but I just don't know. Was I stupid to beat him at H-O-R-S-E?

Mrs. Potter: If a boy can't handle getting beaten by a girl, that's his problem. Just be yourself, honey.

Narrator: Of course, I ignored her advice. I went back to the gym the next Saturday and let Eric beat me. It didn't make him fall in love with me, though. I talked to Mom about that too.

Maisie: I blew it, Mom. I lost to Eric on purpose. I feel gross.

Mrs. Potter: Honey, let's go to the pet shop. You can pick out something cute. You deserve it. You've had a very hard month.

Narrator: I looked at kittens and puppies. None of them seemed quite right. Then I saw a guy buying a cute-looking rat to feed to his snake. I had to save it.

Maisie: Um, excuse me. I'll take that rat.

Narrator: Mom was shocked when she saw

the rat, but she got over it.

Maisie: I'm naming her Bernadette.

Mrs. Potter: That's a nice name.

Why did Maisie's mother want to cheer Maisie up?

Scene 8

Narrator: At practice on Monday I was still in a bad mood. I wasn't really trying. But I still pinned Beans Agway, a guy two weight classes above me. Everybody was cheering. Then I flashed back to the last game of H-O-R-S-E I'd played with Eric. I realized what had been going on for a long time. The boys were all letting me win.

Maisie: Hey! You're cheering for Agway—not me! Mr. Cappelli, I want the nutcracker!

Cappelli: Forget it.

Narrator: In the nutcracker, one person wrestles ten people in a row for 30 seconds— or until somebody gets pinned.

Maisie: No, you forget it. I need to make them accept me. Your way doesn't work. I'm just a joke to them.

Narrator: Agway was laughing, so I shoved him. Mr. Cappelli grabbed my arm.

Maisie: Nutcracker or I quit!

Cappelli (*quietly*): OK.

Narrator: This time the guys practically fought to wrestle me. Agway was first. He pinned me in a couple of seconds.

Kruko: You're stupid, Agway. You should have kept it going.

Narrator: Kruko, all 145 pounds of him, was next. He didn't beat me right away. He took the full 30 seconds.

Cappelli: That's 30 seconds. Next!

Narrator: After that, it's blurry. I wrestled ten guys. In the end, Mr. Cappelli had to revive me with smelling salts.

Cappelli: Are you OK, Tiger?

Maisie: Yeah.

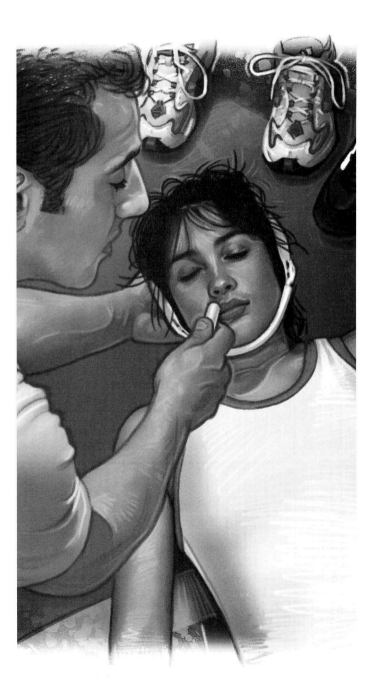

Narrator: I heard clapping and wondered why. Then I realized people were cheering for me. Even Agway and Kruko. Mr. Cappelli asked me some questions to make sure I was OK. Then he got real serious.

Cappelli: I don't know whether to be mad at you—or at myself—for letting you get away with that. I'll be satisfied as long as you can walk out of here tonight. This is as new to me as it is to you. I let you do that because I thought something drastic was called for. I didn't have any better ideas.

Narrator: Then he sighed and sent me to the locker room. Tina McIntyre was in there changing. I must not have looked too good.

Tina: What happened to you?!

Narrator: Tall Tina was our girls' basketball star. We'd been friendly when we played together the year before. But we weren't really friends off the court.

Tina: There's blood on your sweatshirt, and your lip's as big as...

Narrator: I was trying to take my shoes off. But I couldn't manage it. Tina helped me.

Tina: I hope you're not doing this for him.

Narrator: She helped me get the rest of my clothes off. Then she shoved me in the direction of the shower.

Tina: That's as far as I go.

Narrator: Mr. Cappelli had George wait for me outside the locker room. He and Tina walked me home.

Maisie *(to George)*: Now I know why you wouldn't wrestle me. You didn't want to join in the little joke.

Tina: You could have told her what they were doing. *(after a pause)* So, George. You think she's going to catch loverboy Delong? Think he's worth it?

Narrator: I kicked Tina in the shins. George didn't say anything.

Tina: I hope it's not about Eric. I hope she's doing it just to be outrageous!

Narrator: We'd reached my house. I went inside, fed Bernadette, and fell asleep. I woke up when I felt a hand on my fat lip. I opened my eyes. It was my little sister, P.K., and a kid I'd never seen before.

P.K.: Hi, Maisie! This is my friend Tank. He wants to touch your lip.

Maisie: Yo, Tank.

P.K.: Tank wants to see you wrestle. Can we?

Narrator: So P.K. and Tank started coming to practice every day. That meant I had three friends: a rat and two 5-year-olds.

Why do you think Maisie stays on the wrestling team?

Scene 9

Narrator: Our first match was after the semester break. When my turn came, I headed for the mat.

Cappelli: You can do it, Maisie.

Narrator: My opponent didn't come to the mat. His coach motioned for Mr. Cappelli to meet him at the timer's table.

Cappelli: I was afraid of this.

Narrator: Then the announcer said, "In the l05-pound class we have a forfeit. The winner is Maisie Potter."

Narrator: The next morning, P.K. ran into my bedroom with the newspaper.

P.K.: You're famous, Maisie!

Maisie *(reading a headline):* "There's a Girl in My Hammerlock." That's so stupid.

Narrator: The letters to the editor later that week were worse than the silly little story. Tina came over after school the day they were printed.

Tina: People are fools. Listen to this: "When I opened your paper and saw a picture of a male and female wrestling, I was shocked. How could the school allow this?"

Maisie: I got a note on my locker like that.

Tina: Listen. There's a dance at school tonight. Let's go. It'll be good for you.

Narrator: But it turned out to be a huge disaster. Someone put a sign up that said "Hunkiest Boy at the Dance: Eric Delong. Runner-up: Maisie Potter." The next day was our second wrestling match. The other team forfeited again. The same thing happened the next week. At the fourth match, the other team's coach weighed me in.

Maisie: So, are you guys going to forfeit?

Coach: Hey! We're no chickens.

Maisie *(smiling)*: All right!

Narrator: The noise was amazing when I trotted out to the mat. Some people were cheering. A lot more were booing.

Cappelli: Here you go. It's what you've been waiting for. You can do it, Maisie.

Narrator: I hit the floor running—and got pinned in 22 seconds. But I was so happy to wrestle that I didn't care that I lost.

Kruko and Bamberger: Nice try.

Narrator: After my match, the cheering went on and on. But the match was at home. My own school was happy that I lost. I didn't feel so good anymore. Once we got home, my parents tried to cheer me up.

Mrs. Potter: Not everybody was cheering—just a couple of nitwits.

Maisie *(upset):* Until I heard them, I didn't mind getting pinned.

Mr. Potter: Back in the principal's office, you

said you wouldn't care. Your coach tried to tell you . . .

Maisie *(almost crying):* Yeah, but I didn't count on being voted the hunkiest boy at the dance! I didn't count on having my own friends cheer against me. Dad, you're always so big on being fair. Well, this isn't fair! And it isn't easy.

Narrator: I ran up the stairs to my room. My mother called after me.

Mrs. Potter: We know.

Narrator: People kept writing to the paper about how I was unnatural. But Tina became my friend. That was the one good thing.

Maisie: I'm at the point where the only time I'm happy is during the actual bouts.

Tina: That's about two minutes a week.

Maisie: Yeah. It would be nice if I could last beyond the first period for once.

Narrator: Against Upper Jonesford, I finally did. I still lost, but not until 20 seconds into the second period. I saw Tina afterwards.

Tina: I loved that chant they did in the stands: "Potter, Potter, she's our man..."

Maisie: Yeah, I heard it.

Tina: And did you hear this? Eric and Lizard broke up.

Narrator: And I was still shocked when I answered the phone Thursday.

Eric: Want to go out tomorrow?

Maisie: OK.

Eric: OK. Bye.

Narrator: I wondered where we'd go and what we'd do. Then I worried that he wouldn't call back. But he did.

Eric: Meet me at Shirts Plus at 7 o'clock.

Maisie: OK.

Narrator: Dad drove me to the mall. It was snowing, and I worried that the whole thing would fall through. I didn't know if Eric would be there when I got to Shirts Plus. He was.

Eric: Hi. Let's go to the arcade.

Narrator: He demolished me at video games. Then we went to the pizzeria. Eric and I sat down and had a slice.

Eric: My brother is at the mall, too. We drove here in his Mustang convertible.

Maisie *(smiling):* Not with the top down today, I hope.

Eric: Nah, but I wanted to. Want to go sit in it? I have a key. We can listen to music.

Maisie: OK.

Narrator: He put his arm around me, and we trudged through the snowy parking lot. In the car, Eric played a new CD.

Eric: Do you hear that? This stereo's got quadraphonic sound!

Narrator: Then suddenly he was on me. His lips mashed against my teeth. My head hit the door. My shoe got stuck in the steering wheel. And I punched him. It's hard to explain why. Maybe I was just shocked. I

wanted it to be last summer, at the swimming pool. I wanted to start over. I could almost hear myself shouting *Not this way! Not yet!* And I punched him again.

Eric: Hey! What are you doing?

Maisie *(yelling):* What are *you* doing?

Eric: I thought you liked me!

Maisie: I did.

Narrator: But I didn't anymore. I got out of the car. I ran to the phone in the mall.

Maisie *(to her dad)*: Pick me up! Now!

Narrator: When I got home, Mom, P.K., and Tank were in the living room. They looked at me really strangely. It was as if they had been waiting for me. But they couldn't know what had happened to me. Or could they? I didn't want to talk about it. So I went up to my room. I'd play with Bernadette, my rat. She'd make me feel better.

Maisie: Where is Bernadette? Bernadette!!

Narrator: She wasn't there. She was missing. Moments later, my mother and sister and Tank were in my room.

Mrs. Potter: I'm sorry, Maisie. I let P.K. and Tank play with Bernadette downstairs. Tank accidentally let her out the door. She's gone.

P.K.: It wasn't Tank's fault. Don't be mad.

Maisie *(yelling):* Oh, I'm not mad. I just had

the worst night of my life. Then I come home and find out my rat's gone. *(moving toward Tank)* And it's your fault!

Narrator: I was sorry as soon as I said it. Tank ran out the door and into the street. I followed him. Just then, a snowplow turned the corner. It was bearing down on Tank. I made a flying leap and scooped Tank out of its way. I threw him toward the house.

Maisie *(to herself):* Please, please land in the snow.

Narrator: Then the plow's blade picked me up.

How did Maisie save Tank?

Scene 10

Narrator: I woke up in the hospital.

Mrs. Potter: You're going to be OK.

Maisie: The snowplow hit me. Is Tank . . .

Mrs. Potter: Tank's fine. Perfect.

Narrator: I had bruises and a concussion. But basically I was OK. I went home the next day. And guess what? Bernadette was there, too.

Mrs. Potter: The mailman found her in the mailbox. I don't know how she got in there.

Narrator: Mr. Cappelli came to visit.

Cappelli: Everyone on the team stopped by to ask me how you were doing.

Maisie: Not Kruko?

Cappelli: Even Kruko.

Narrator: Then Mr. Cappelli gave me a get-well banner that the whole team had signed. I was also in the paper that day. The article told about my "daring rescue" of Tank. The next time I was in the paper was our last bout of the season. There was a photo of the crowd cheering as the team carried me off the mat. I had gone three full periods against my opponent. I never won. But by the end, I had people's approval. The funny thing is that by then I didn't need it. I had the approval of the person who counted most: Me.

How do you feel about Maisie?

Meet the Author

When I was growing up, the first thing I wanted to be was a cowboy. Then I wanted to be a baseball player. I played Little League in junior high and high school. I only hit two home runs in my career.

Around that time, our high school team won a heart-stopping game against one of the best teams in the country. A few days later, the poem I had written about it was published in the local newspaper. Suddenly I had something new to become: a writer.

My ideas come from everyday life. And from the newspapers. One day, for example, I read a story about a girl who competed on her high school wrestling team. A year later bookstores carried a new book with my name on it: *There's a Girl in My Hammerlock*.

Wheel Trouble

Patrick Daley and Chuck Ranberg

SCHOLASTIC INC.
New York Toronto London Auckland Sydney
Mexico City New Delhi Hong Kong

**Cover illustration by
Gurmita Singh**

**Interior illustrations by
Peter Spacek**

Characters

Narrator, Scott recalling the events

Scott Wheeler, a high school student

Mr. Wheeler, Scott's father

Mrs. Stevenson, Scott's teacher

Spike, Scott's friend

Carol, Scott's girlfriend

Rocco Rocovitch, Scott's enemy

Stacy, Rocco's girlfriend

Al B., Scott's gym buddy

Scene 1

Narrator: Dad was a pretty reasonable guy. Except when it came to cars. I felt I needed one. He felt I didn't. That night at dinner, I was ready with my 100th plan to get some wheels. I called it Mission Ignition.

Scott: Dad, I've been thinking.

Mr. Wheeler: Really? How unusual.

Narrator: Dad sometimes gets carried away with his sarcasm.

Scott: Seriously, Dad, I was thinking that I could be more help to you around here if I had my own car. I could help with errands and...

Mr. Wheeler *(interrupting):* I've been thinking

too, Scott. Actually it was the letter I got from your school today that really got me thinking.

Narrator: Suddenly, I felt Mission Ignition turning into Mission Impossible.

Scott *(nervously):* Oh, really? What did the school want? Did you win the Father-of-the-Year contest I nominated you for?

Mr. Wheeler: Not quite. They wrote to say that you are dangerously close to failing English this term.

Narrator: I explained why my Shakespeare report never quite got finished. It was a good excuse, too. One of my better ones.

Mr. Wheeler: Scott, never put off until tomorrow what you can do today.

Narrator: Dad had a saying for all occasions.

Scott: But Dad, what if...

Mr. Wheeler: No "what ifs," Scott. What if I didn't do my job? I wouldn't get paid. Simple as that. Until you pass English, not only are you not getting your own car, but the family

car is off-limits, too.

Scott: But, Dad...

Mr. Wheeler: No "buts," either. When you get out into the real world, you'll find excuses won't pay the rent.

Narrator: I hated it when Dad talked about the "real world." What did he think high school was—a fairy-tale world?

Why won't Scott's dad let him get a car?

Scene

Narrator: The next day in English class, I was having this great daydream: There I was, driving this classic Corvette convertible. The sun was shining, the radio was blasting, and Stacy, the cheerleader who dumped me years ago, was waving to me from the corner. Slowly, I...

Mrs. Stevenson: Earth to Scott. Would you care to answer the question?

Narrator: Suddenly, I had no daydream. I had no car. And I had no idea what my teacher was talking about.

Scott: Uh... could you repeat that?

Narrator: The whole class laughed.

Mrs. Stevenson: Never mind. It's time to

begin term projects. And for some of you, it's your last chance to pull up your grades.

Narrator: Was it my imagination, or was Mrs. Stevenson staring right at me?

Mrs. Stevenson: I want 10 pages about any topic. Then you'll present what you've learned to the class. And for some of you *(looking at Scott again),* this grade could make the difference between passing and failing this class.

Narrator: Clearly, Mrs. Stevenson thought "some of us" were in deep trouble. I vowed I would start my project that night.

Why does Scott need to do well on this project?

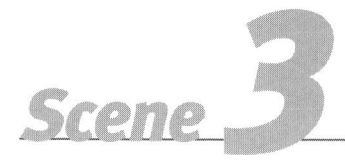 

Scene 3

Narrator: By sundown, however, I still hadn't come up with a good topic. I thought getting some fresh air might stimulate my brain. So I called my girlfriend, Carol, to see if she'd go downtown with me.

Scott: Dad, can I borrow the car?

Mr. Wheeler: You mean, "May I" borrow the car, English expert?

Scott: OK, may I borrow the car?

Mr. Wheeler: You may not.

Narrator: Carol and I took the bus downtown to Java Joe's, where our friend Spike worked.

Spike: Yo, lovebirds. What brings you to Java

Joe's? Public transportation, I presume.

Carol: Careful, Spike. Scott's not in the mood for jokes today.

Spike: Sorry, man. School troubles...again?

Narrator: I explained my newest school crisis, and how I couldn't think of a good topic.

Carol: How about the 2000 election?

Scott: Too boring.

Spike: The environment?

Scott: Too big.

Carol: Outer space.

Scott: Really too big.

Spike: I've got it! How about studying how baby cockroaches feed off dead skin cells?

Carol: That's gross.

Spike: True, but they're small.

Narrator: At that moment, a cherry-red Camaro roared into the parking lot. It was Rocco Rocovitch, the biggest jock in school. He'd been my enemy since freshman year. He had humiliated me in gym class. He had the car of my dreams. And he was going out with Stacy, the ex-girl of my dreams.

Rocco: Hey, Wheeler, did you have a good nap in English today?

Scott: Not as good as the nap you took during the eighth grade.

Rocco: Someday that mouth of yours is going to get you in trouble, Wheeler.

Narrator: Rocco had seen eighth grade more

than once. It was a sore subject.

Stacy: Forget it, Rocco. He's not worth it.

Carol: He is too!

Scott: Uh, Carol, I think I'd better handle this. *(to Rocco)* Do you have a topic for your English project yet?

Rocco: Sure. I'm going to make a timeline showing all your dating disasters over the past four years. Stacy's helping me with the research!

Narrator: The two comedians left, laughing.

Spike: Wow, you'd better get busy. Even Rocco has a topic!

Scott: I'll figure something out. Tomorrow.

Why doesn't Scott like Rocco?

Scene 4

Narrator: A few days later, I still hadn't come up with a topic. I decided that a good workout might get the blood flowing to my brain. So I called my friend Al B. and met him at the gym.

Al B.: Sounds like you are seriously avoiding your project, dude.

Narrator: I could feel the need for a good excuse bubbling inside.

Scott: Not true. I just haven't found a good topic yet.

Al B.: Scott, take a look around the gym. Everyone here has one thing in common. Do you know what it is?

Scott: Body odor?

Al B.: Speak for yourself. Everyone here isn't sitting at home talking about being physically fit. They're doing it. If you want to pass English, you've got to stop complaining and start doing. Just do it, man.

Narrator: Al B. had seen too many sneaker commercials for his own good, but I knew he was right. It was time for me to get with the program.

Do you agree with Al B.'s advice to Scott? Why or why not?

 **Scene 5**

Narrator: As I was walking home, I saw a cherry-red Camaro parked on the side of the road. Its hood was up, and underneath it was Rocco.

Scott: Hey, Rocco, need some help?

Narrator: Not that I cared about him. It's just that, how could anyone not help a beautiful Camaro in distress?

Rocco: No thanks, Wheeler. This is a man's job. Something you wouldn't know about.

Narrator: I tried once more.

Scott: Do you think it's the battery?

Rocco: Beats me.

Scott: Did you check the spark-plug wires?

Camaros often have trouble with them. They get loose sometimes.

Rocco: Really? How do you know all this?

Scott: I read a lot about cars. You see, in my house, you can't own a car. You can only read about them.

Narrator: Rocco liked my joke. And better yet, I was right about the spark-plug wires. In minutes, the car was running smoothly.

Rocco: Thanks, Wheeler. Need a ride home?

Narrator: As we drove, we talked about cars, girls, and even English projects.

Scott: So Rocco, is your project finished yet?

Narrator: I wanted to be sure he wasn't really writing about my dating disasters.

Rocco: Finished? Man, I don't even have a topic yet. I can't seem to get started.

Narrator: I tried to hide my relief. Who would've thought Rocco and I would ever have something in common?

Narrator: Later that night, I sat down one

more time to come up with a topic for my project. But it was no use. I thought about everything else, working out with Al B. and working on Rocco's car. Then it hit me!

Scott: Rocco!

Narrator: I picked up the phone. I dialed and waited for Rocco to answer.

Rocco: What's up, Wheeler?

Scott: Call me crazy. But I think I have an idea that's worth talking about. It could jump-start both of our grades.

What do you think Scott's idea is?

Scene 6

Narrator: Two weeks later in English class, Rocco and I made our presentation.

Scott: So you see, by following these steps, you can avoid most car problems.

Rocco: And if you do have problems, this checklist and guide we wrote should help. We have copies for everyone.

Narrator: Afterward, everyone had a question about car repairs and emergencies on the road.

Mrs. Stevenson: I'm impressed. You two have obviously done a lot of research.

Scott: Yeah, well, it's easy when you pick something you like learning about.

Rocco *(giving Scott a thumbs-up)*: And I learned that Wheeler here isn't such a loser, after all.

Narrator: That Rocco—what a charmer.

How did Scott and Rocco solve their problem?

Scene 7

Narrator: Rocco and I got an "A" on our project. When report cards came out, I was pleased to show mine to Dad. He was pleased, too.

Mr. Wheeler: I'm very proud of you, son.

Scott: Yeah. And...

Mr. Wheeler: You can start using the family car again.

Scott: Yeah. And...

Mr. Wheeler: I've been thinking about you having your own car.

Narrator: This was getting good.

Scott: Yeah. And...

Mr. Wheeler: If...

Narrator: Uh-oh, trouble.

Mr. Wheeler: If you continue to do well, we'll look into a reasonably priced, dependable used car.

Narrator: Good-bye, Camaro. Hello, jalopy.

Scott: But Dad, why put off until tomorrow what you can do today?

Mr. Wheeler: Because I'm a parent.

Narrator: Parents. Don't even try to figure them out.

What made Scott's dad change his mind about letting Scott have a car?

Meet the Authors

I live in New York and work in publishing. Chuck lives in Los Angeles and writes for TV sitcoms. Chuck's won two Emmys for episodes he's worked on. I haven't won any. (They don't have Emmys in *my* business.)

People sometimes ask how Chuck and I—on opposite sides of the country—hooked up to write *Wheel Trouble* and some other plays. Well, years ago, he and I shared a house with a bunch of friends. We soon discovered that we shared similar (and painful) memories of first jobs, mean gym teachers, and disastrous school projects.

So, Chuck and I started writing these plays. First, we'd bounce a bunch of funny ideas and jokes off each other. Some worked—and some didn't. Now when the two of us want to collaborate, we have to do it long distance. That's when the phone bills get nasty—for him. I call collect!

—*Patrick Daley and Chuck Ranberg*